Nonviolent Communication
The Basics As I Know And Use Them

D1600278

WAYLAND MYERS, PH.D.

Nonviolent Communication

The Basics As I Know and Use Them

Published By Wayland Myers,
645 Cole Ranch Road, Encinitas, CA,
92024, USA

Printed in United States
Designed by Atelier Weidmann - Switzerland
Cover Artwork by J.-C. Marol

Acknowledgments

I am deeply grateful to
> Marshall Rosenberg for creating, developing and sharing the communication process I attempt to describe in this book;
> to Lucy Leu and other Nonviolent Communication trainers for helping me refine some of the technical points;
> to Barbara Grant for helping me improve the quality of my writing;
> and to Allan Adelman, Nicolee McMahon, Helen Myers and other good friends for their steady encouragement, support and faith.

I am grateful to have been able to create this book in the company of people I enjoy and value so much.

Table of Contents

Foreword

Marshall Rosenberg's Nonviolent Communication process is largely a language of the heart and he sometimes calls it the language of "Giraffe." Giraffes have the largest hearts of any land animal, long necks that allow them to see the big picture and they regularly stick out their necks in the service of life.

The tree images used in this book are Acacias, a favorite food of giraffes.

Marshall has named those analytic and diagnostic forms of speaking that often result in hurt or violence the language of "Jackal." In English, a jackal often connotes a person of disreputable character, usually held in low esteem. However, as the photo on the next page clearly demonstrates, this may be an unearned and unwarranted association. If this jackal could speak, the author believes that he would express the pain and confusion he feels that his species—so obviously cute, adorable and precious, would be used in such an uncomplimentary, iconic manner. The author empathizes with his pain.

☐

Preface

"Several years ago I shared a process I call Nonviolent Communication with Wayland Myers. I was pleased when he later told me how Nonviolent Communication enriched his personal and professional life. And now, when I read his book explaining how he was able to do this, I am confident that readers will benefit from his experience with the process. His clarity and humor contribute to making important concepts easily accessible without over simplification. I am very pleased with this book."

MARSHALL ROSENBERG

[Ender, the Speaker for the Dead, talking to his son] "...when it comes to human beings, the only type of cause that matters is final cause, the purpose. What a person has in mind. Once you understand what people really want, you can't hate them anymore. You can fear them, but you can't hate them, because you can always find the same desires in your own heart."

Speaker for the Dead, Orson Scott Card

□

This statement intrigues me. The Speaker says that it is possible to hate or fear the methods a person uses to achieve a goal, but hard to hate the person's deepest motives because they are ones we have known, or can imagine, within ourselves.

I find myself pausing to take this in, then deepening my contemplation to another level: **is every human act—mental, emotional or physical—an attempt by the actor to sustain or improve the quality or longevity of his or her life?** If this is true, then I don't know how to dislike this motive or its author. I know how to dislike, object, reject or even attempt to restrict the author's means or methods, but not the fundamental drive.

I know that it is true that at one time or another, all of us try to get our needs met by acting in ways which others find harmful, painful, even life threatening. Some of us do this intentionally and habitually. During these moments, I believe that a number of things may be true:

○ We may not know a better means to achieve our ends.

○ We may not see the harm that follows from our actions, or recognize how that harm brings loss to us.

○ We may have behavioral compulsions that we find hard to resist.

○ Or, we may be convinced that ours are the only or best methods.

All of this notwithstanding, it still appears true to me that everything we humans do is an attempt to sustain or improve the quality or continuity of our lives. If this is so, then we all share and live from a common ground.

I have discovered that if I keep this possibility in the foreground of my mind when relating to myself and others, I often experience a natural and powerful sense of compassion that is infused with a deep feeling of communion. Marshall Rosenberg's Nonviolent Communication has played a central role in opening me to this experience and helps me enjoy it on a daily basis. In fact, I would say that helping people jointly develop and enhance this deep sense of compassionate communion is what Nonviolent Communication is mainly about.

□

Nonviolent Communication

If the word "violent" means acting in ways that result in hurt or harm, then much of how we communicate with ourselves and each other could be called violent. For example, when we say things like, "You make me angry or crazy," or "You hurt my feelings," we are declaring that others are responsible for our thoughts and emotions. This can leave us feeling resentful and hopeless, and our listeners feeling angry or guilty. And, when we speak about how we are and what we need by using moralistic labels like, "That was selfish, stupid, cruel, irresponsible, etc.," we often leave ourselves feeling sad and lonely, and our listeners feeling hurt or afraid. Guilt, fear, anger, loneliness, resentment, sadness—all are forms of pain: To the extent that our customary methods of communication tend to elicit them, these forms of communication can be called violent.

When I think about the depth and breadth of human suffering that is the byproduct of our usual forms of communication, I feel sad. It doesn't matter to me that this pain is usually unintentional. And, when I think about the vast amount of energy we spend dealing with these distressful emotions, I realize that our most familiar methods of communication cost us a great deal. They seem to be based on the belief that we humans often need coercion and control in order to become motivated. Until 1986, I knew of no alternatives. Then I met Dr. Marshall Rosenberg and he introduced me to his Nonviolent Communication process. Now I relate to myself and others in profoundly different ways.

The Purpose of the Process

I view Nonviolent Communication as both an attitude and a set of tools that are especially designed to help me realize and enjoy a deep truth: *That every day, in every act, we are all motivated by the same need*—**the need to sustain or improve the quality or continuity of our lives**. Nonviolent Communication encourages us to take the time to explore our motives deeply, to work with commitment, compassion and creativity and assures us that by doing so we will often invent ways of proceeding which enable each of us realize our dreams simultaneously. It provides practical tools to help us acheive this.

Through its methods and insights Nonviolent Communication helps me not only feel compassion for and linked to all living creatures, but it helps me know how to express this compassion in my actions. Doing this I experience deep joy, inspiration and nourishment, and am blessed with many more friends. I wish you similar joys.

Although Nonviolent Communication can be, and is, powerfully applied to help us relate to *ourselves* with increased compassion, this primer is focused more on its interpersonal applications. Within the interpersonal sphere, Nonviolent Communication's intent is to help people interact in ways that leave all parties feeling more whole within and connected together, and where their motivations for helping themselves and each other are not fear, obligation or guilt, but because helping becomes the most fulfilling activity they can imagine.

Guides, Not Rules

When first exposed to Dr. Rosenberg's process I thought of it as a way of speaking and convinced myself that I *should* speak this way all the time. Family and friends still remember the obnoxious nature of that experience. Often I heard, "Can't you just talk normal?" And, of course, I didn't just try to make myself speak this way. I also "subtly" implied that everyone else should speak this way too. I was a lot of fun.

Today my family and friends feel grateful for the evolution in my understanding and practice. I now understand that Nonviolent Communication is not a way of speaking, but more *an attitude and a set of concepts and tools designed to help people establish a certain kind of compassionate rapport with themselves and each other.* The special nature of this rapport is that, when it is present and sustained, people often become spontaneously willing to do what they can to meet their own and each other's needs.

I encourage you to view the concepts and tools I am about to share as *guides* or aids to help you generate compassion, generosity and a sense of communion with yourself and others, not as *rules* to follow. In the beginning, you may rely on them heavily, as you would training wheels, to help you learn to speak and listen in the ways most likely to inspire compassion. But, if you use them too rigidly or dogmatically, they can impede the creation of the very compassion you seek. My recommendation: Use them like training wheels in the beginning, but then learn to use them more like a pilot's checklist—a device which helps you remember important points and procedures, and helps solve common problems, but is not meant to tell you how to fly or govern your every move. The primary intent of Nonviolent Communication is to enable people

to relate to themselves and each other in ways
which inspire compassion, connection and generosity, not to create a new social subgroup that
speaks an idiomatic language.

□

What to Share and Listen For: Two Basic Questions

One of Nonviolent Communication's goals is to help people communicate in ways that enable all parties to become compassionately inspired to do what they can to meet their own and each other's needs. Dr. Rosenberg has found that encouraging us to talk about the state of our well-being, and what could be done to improve it, is one of the most useful things we can do.

Therefore, in Nonviolent Communication there are two general questions we try to answer for each party:

"How am I doing?"
(How are *you* doing) and,

**"What can be done *now* to improve
my well-being? (your well-being?)"**

If both of us are trained in the process, we can work together to answer these questions for each other. If only one of us knows the process, that person can guide the conversation so that these questions are answered for both. It is **not** required that each party be trained in or committed to using Nonviolent Communication.

We can provide details for the **"How am I doing?"** question by furnishing each other with three simple pieces of information:

① What **event** is triggering each person's desire to talk: What is being seen, sensed, heard, thought, recalled,...?

② What **emotions** are stirred within each person: fear, excitement, anger, hurt, curiosity,...?

③ What **personal needs** are the source of those emotions: the need for safety, nourishment, information, companionship, respect, understanding, choice,...?

We can answer the **"What can be done now to improve my well-being?"** question by providing each other with a fourth piece of information:

④ **What specific actions** would anyone like to perform, or have another perform, **right now**: listen, explain, problem solve, agree to act,...?

I find it useful to think of these four pieces of information as a *checklist*. Let's look at them individually.

Triggering Events

Prior to the beginning of a conversation, something happens which triggers a person's desire to communicate. Something is experienced, seen, heard, thought, felt, sensed, smelled, recalled, etc. Since this is the origin of the urge to communicate it often helps if everyone knows what it is.

Emotions

By becoming aware of our emotions, and other internal sensations (like hunger, fatigue and thirst), we come to know how we are doing. Our emotions and sensations inform us about the status of our needs. Pleasurable emotions, like joy, excitement or delight, tell us that some of our needs have been met or we believe they will be. Painful emotions, like fear, anger, sadness, hurt or embarrassment, tell us that some of our needs aren't met, or we believe they won't be. Given the valuable information that emotions provide regarding the status of our well-being, and that they are the driving force behind our behavior, the identification of emotions plays a central role in conveying how we are doing. But, just identifying emotions is not enough.

Personal Needs
(Desires, Dreams, Appetites, etc.)

Because our emotions are intimately linked to our needs, it is easier to accurately understand each other's emotions if information about the underlying needs is made available. For example, right now I feel happy and content. But, you may not understand the particular nature of my happiness unless I tell you which of my needs is involved and what I am thinking about them. In this case, I am happy because I have a need to help others bring more compassion into their lives and by working on this small book I believe that I'm doing just that. This combination of what I am needing and believing produces my emotion. Telling you about it helps you better understand this particular happiness. However, a few minutes ago, I was also happy. But then, I was happy because I experienced a need for companionship and when I called a friend, I heard that he would be glad to speak right then.

My point is this, our emotions are the result of an interaction between our needs, our thoughts and the sensory information we have available. If we want to keenly understand each other's emotions, it helps to clearly articulate the needs, thoughts and sensory information that are producing them.

There is a second benefit that comes from identifying the needs linked to each person's emotions. Because of the vulnerability and common humanity that we reveal when we articulate the needs we want fulfilled, or the dreams we wish to realize, others can identify with us and they often feel a spontaneous sense of communion and a compassionate generosity. That is, when we have needs and dreams in want of fulfillment we demonstrate a kind of universally recognizable vulnerability that others can identify with and which often inspires them to *spontaneously respond in helpful ways.* I value this insight highly.

Actions Desired

It often happens that after learning how someone is via the first three checklist items, a listener may wonder if the speaker wants to take any particular action now, or wants the listener to do anything right then. Therefore, the fourth checklist item involves identifying a specific action, if there is one, which someone could do now that might meet an immediate need of the person making the request.

This information forms a natural bridge to the next round of communication which often involves learning how the other person is doing, what they need, and how their needs make it easier or harder for them to do what we ask.

Checklist Examples

The following dialogs illustrate a speaker sharing all four pieces of information with another. In that they follow a structured form of speaking, these are "training wheel" types of examples. You can gradually learn how to share and gather this information in less formula-like ways.

"When I got your invitation [*receiving the invitation was **the event***],

I was excited [***an emotion***],

because I love doing things with people I enjoy [***the need** for companionship and play is producing the emotion*].

Could you tell me who else will be coming [***a request** for specific information*]?"

"When I heard that you had lost your job [*hearing is **the event***],

I was sad [***an emotion***],

because I want you to have a job you love and I know you loved that one [*the listener is sad because they have **a need** for the person to whom they are speaking to be happily employed*].

Would you care to talk to me about how this is affecting you [*the speaker **requests** specific information*]?"

"I was really annoyed [***an emotion***]

when I heard you describe me as 'lazy' [*hearing oneself described as lazy is **the event***],

because I prefer that people tell me what they want, but aren't getting from me, rather than what they think of me [*the unmet **need** is for per-*

32

sonal disclosure on the part of the person who used the term 'lazy'].

Would you tell me what need or desire of yours didn't get fulfilled that motivated you to call me 'lazy' [*a **request** for specific information*]?"

A Nonviolent Communication conversation often consists of a rhythmic series of these exchanges—how I am and what I want, followed by how you are and what you want, followed by how I am, etc., continued until everyone's needs are met as much as possible or we agree that we've done the best we can.

□

How to Share
and Listen:
Three Recommendations

At this point you may be recalling that there have been many times when you told another how you were and what you wanted, and yet it didn't turn out well. You didn't end up feeling compassionate, connected or generous toward each other. In fact, you often ended feeling more disappointed, hurt, angry and frustrated. I have too. Obviously, there something more we need to do than just identify our triggering events, and express our emotions and needs. The key seems to be in **how** we talk and listen to each other about these things.

Nonviolent Communication makes some suggestions in this regard which I distill into three recommendations. We are encouraged to do the following:

① **Describe** events, emotions and needs ***without*** using evaluative judgments, moralistic labels or name-calling.

② Avoid blaming or behaving defensively. **Developing a deeper understanding of the personal needs which are producing each person's emotions and choices** is often more productive.

③ **When making requests, be specific** about the behaviors that each person would like themselves or another to do right now. Avoid trying to get anyone's needs met through demands, threats and guilt or shaming manipulations.

Let's explore these suggestions.

Describe Facts
Don't Name-call or Moralize

This first recommendation acknowledges that most of us don't like it when others tell us what they think is right or wrong with us or our actions. So it says, when talking about what is happening, felt or needed, **describe** it **objectively** rather than offering moralistic or evaluative opinions about it. Opinions of value, worthiness, appropriateness, etc. tend to stimulate defensiveness and unproductive debate whereas *descriptions of facts* tend to be adjusted only for completeness or accuracy.

For example, when trying to identify the triggering event, if I say, "When *you lie* to me," that can be perceived as my way of moralistically labeling what you did. However, if I say, "When your description of what happened doesn't match what I hear from others," that is a simple, objective description of what I experienced. Or when talking about my feelings, if I say, "I feel you're *irresponsible*," again that is my way of morally characterizing your behavior, whereas, "I'm feeling anger and disappointment," is a description of my emotions. (A caution: phrases

Translating Opinions into Descriptions of Facts

might become

You ripped me off.	When my stuff was taken without my permission.
You acted like a wimp.	When you did not act.
That is a stupid idea.	I feel uncomfortable with your proposal.
When you were rude.	When you began talking while I was speaking.
I feel you are disrespectfull.	I feel angry, hurt and sad.
I feel so stupid.	When I think about what I did, I feel embarrassment.
You are an idiot.	When I see how this turned out I feel angry.

Making these kinds of translations is one of the primary tasks performed in Nonviolent Communication.

beginning with "I feel I..., I feel you, he/she, we, they, one, it, ..., or I feel that ..." all herald the coming of an opinion.) *In Nonviolent Communication we try to translate all of the opinions we hear, or want to express, into* **objective descriptions** of what was done, observed or happened.

This is accomplished by asking oneself a simple question, "*What actually happened, or was done or observed, that is being* **labeled as** *stupid, rude, abusive, dishonest, etc.?*" The examples in the table to the left illustrate this point.

Illuminate Feelings and Needs
Avoid Blaming or Defending

Many of us have learned to explain our emotions and actions by denying personal responsibility for them and/or blaming them on the behavior of others. We say things like, "You *make* me mad (happy, sad, etc.)," "I had *no choice* but to..." or "I *couldn't* help feeling..." These are actually forms of blaming and often provoke fruitless debate.

Too Little Information	Statements Blaming Others	Statements that Reveal the Speaker's Needs
I feel hurt.	I feel hurt *because you* left me out.	I am hurting *because I* like to be included.
I am angry.	You *made me* angry when you stole my bike from me.	I am angry *because I* want to grant permission for someone to use my bike.
I am sad.	I am sad *because you* aren't affectionate.	I am sad and lonely *because I* am longing to be held.
You asked for it.	When you did that *I had no choice* but to leave you.	I left you *because I* needed time alone to sort through my feelings.
I had to leave.	I had to leave *because they* were behaving badly.	I left *because I* needed to reduce my stress.

It is true that our feelings and choices are *influenced* by the actions of others. What others do provides us with a particular stimulus to respond to. But in my experience, *how* we respond to that stimulus is determined more by how we *think* about what is going on, and what we *need* in relation to it, than by the stimulus itself. Therefore, Nonviolent Communication recommends that we spend our energy exploring how the needs and thoughts of each individual have shaped his or her feelings and choices, rather than trying to assign or debate blame.

○ The table to the left contains statements that don't offer enough information about feelings, actions or needs to promote understanding and compassion;

○ statements that blame others for a person's feelings and actions;

○ and statements that inspire understanding and compassion because they describe how the speaker's needs are producing his or her feelings and behaviors.

The italicized words in the second column emphasize how the speaker is blaming others for his or her feelings or actions. In the third column, the italicized words "*because I*" highlight the fact that all of these phrases point to the *speaker's* inner realities as being the source of his or her emotions, *not* the listener's, or anyone else's behavior. That is, the speaker keeps the focus on him or herself.

Before moving on to the third recommendation, I want to attempt a clarification of the distinction between emotions, needs and requests.

I believe that we learn about our needs *through* our **emotions** and other sensations of sufficiency or deficiency, like hunger, thirst, etc. When our needs are met, we experience the emotions and sensations of fullness, satisfaction, comfort, contentment, etc. When they aren't, we experience grief, yearnings, longings, cravings, hungers or urges.

Our **needs** tend to be *general* and involve *necessities* fundamental to all people. They can be grouped into broad categories like physical (the needs for food, shelter, safety, ...), social (the needs for companionship, affection, ...), political (the needs for freedom of choice, freedom of expression, representation, ...), financial, spiritual, intellectual, etc. If I wanted to speak about my needs I would say things like, "I need affection," "I need food," "I need company," "I need to believe that I am heard," "I need information," or "I need to be able to grant my permission."

A **request**, on the other hand, is *specific*. It is a description of *what we want done* in order for our need to be met. For instance, "Would you be willing to give me a slice of that pizza?" "Will you hold me?" "I want to speak to you now," "I want to vote," "Would you be willing to pay me one hundred dollars tomorrow?"

Nonviolent Communication encourages us to clearly differentiate our needs from our requests because while most of the time people won't object to *what* we need, they often object to the ideas we have about *who, when, where, how much* or *in what way* we want our needs to be met. For instance, if I say, "I need something to drink," most people won't object or debate because they know that I alone have direct access to information regarding what I need. However, if I say, "I would like a drink of your soda," the person I am speaking to may object.

Or, if I say, "I need the reassurance of a deposit," there may be no objection, but if I say, "I want a one thousand dollar deposit," there may be vigorous debate. The point is this: If I want my need to be heard, understood and empathized with, then it is best if I speak about it first, and *separately*, from my request.

There is another important reason for carefully distinguishing between our needs and our requests, and fully illuminating our needs *before* discussing our requests. If we fully explore each person's needs, then it often happens that mutually satisfying ways of proceeding and a spontaneous desire to engage in them emerge *naturally*. That is, as I stated previously, people are often so touched and moved by the vulnerable nature of another's unmet needs and the precious nature of their dreams, that creative and cooperative solutions which enable everyone's needs to be met often form with little effort.

Request Desired Behaviors
Don't Demand, Threaten,
Boss or Manipulate

Nonviolent Communication's third recommendation helps us translate our general needs into specific requests. It recognizes that most of us would prefer that someone tell us precisely what he or she wants rather than command us, threaten us, leave us guessing or try to manipulate us by withdrawing. Therefore the process encourages us to articulate *precisely* the *exact actions* required to meet *our most pressing needs* and to present these in the form of *requests*. It also alerts us to tell people what we *want* them to do, not what we *don't want* them to do. The following chart illustrates these points.

Vague or Intimidating Requests

I want respect.

I want more love. OR You don't love me enough.

I don't need advice.

What's bugging you?

Stop yelling at me. OR I don't want you to yell.

You never listen.

Requests Which Describe Precise Actions

Would you be willing to ask my permission before borrowing my stuff?

Would you be willing to hold me and tell me some of the ways you appreciate me?

I need to sort through my feelings without interruption. Is that OK with you?

Would you be willing to tell me what feelings were triggered in you?

Would you be willing to speak to me to in a softer tone of voice?

Would you be willing to remain silent while I explain to you why I acted that way?

When we express our requests in the ways shown on the right we greatly increase the likelihood of everyone getting exactly what they need, given to them in ways they like.

Nonviolent Communication in Action: Examples

In Nonviolent Communication we are primarily interested in learning how each of us is doing and in discovering what could be done now to improve our respective well-beings. What I call *the checklist* focuses us on certain information that helps us do this and what I call *the three recommendations* helps us communicate about this information in ways most likely to inspire compassion and mutual generosity. Now let's see these two aids working together, but first, here they are in summary.

The Checklist

(1) What **event** is triggering each person's desire to talk: What is being seen, sensed, heard, thought, recalled,...?

(2) What **emotions** are stirred within each person: fear, excitement, anger, hurt, curiosity,...?

(3) What **personal needs** are the source of those emotions: the need for safety, nourishment, information, companionship, respect, understanding, choice,...?

(4) What **specific actions** would anyone like to perform, or have another perform, **right now**: listen, explain, problem solve, agree to act,...?

The Three Recommendations

1. **Describe** events, emotions and needs **without** using evaluative judgments, moralistic labels or name-calling.

2. Avoid blaming or behaving defensively. Instead, **develop a deeper understanding of the personal needs that are producing each person's emotions and choices**.

3. **When making requests, be specific about the behaviors** that each person would like themselves, or another, to do **right now**. Avoid trying to get anyone's needs met through demands, threats and guilt or shaming manipulations.

As I said earlier, we can use the checklist and three recommendations like training wheels to help us when speaking and listening. For instance, *when we speak,* we can ask ourselves which of the checklist's four pieces of information we might need to convey, and we can use the three recommendations to help us communicate that information in ways that are most likely to inspire compassionate understanding, feelings of connection and feelings of generosity. *When we listen,* we can "listen" for the four pieces of information about others and use the three recommendations to help us hear that information in ways most likely to move us compassionately.

The following is a basic example. It is inspired by a conversation I had with a young man who had just left a medical hospital after being treated for a life threatening drug overdose. We were discussing an out-of-state drug rehabilitation program he was about to attend.

Not using the tools

The conversation might have gone this way if I used the "violent" communication methods taught by my culture:

He says to me, "I don't care what the rehab staff says. After four months, I'm coming home."

I blurt out, "You're kidding? You almost died."

With growing agitation in his voice, he says, "I don't care. Four months is enough."

I come back, "You are such a typical alcoholic/addict. Everything's got to be *your* way and in *your* time. If your way is so good, how come you almost died?"

He gets up, head shaking back and forth, angry pain in his voice and says, "Who cares what you think. You're such a jerk." Turning, he leaves the room.

In terms of Nonviolent Communication's concepts what did I do? I didn't reveal to him how I was doing, nor did I learn how he was doing. I implied that he was a fool, which is the same as calling him one. I labeled him an alcoholic/addict.

Responding to him in this way our conversation is short leaving us feeling more isolated and in greater pain—a depressing and common outcome.

Using Nonviolent Communication

The conversation might have gone like this if I used the tools of the process to guide me:

He starts. "I don't care what the rehab staff says. After four months, I'm coming home."

I immediately feel worried and the process tells me that if I want to connect with him in a tangible, constructive way then it may be helpful to get both of us talking about the four facts. I decide to start by sharing the four facts about me.

I say, "I am concerned when I hear you say you're coming home after four months because I want you to get the most and best help you can. Could you tell me more about the feelings or thoughts you have that lead you to say that no matter what anyone else says you are coming home in four months?"

*My hearing him is my **triggering event**. I'm feeling **concerned** because my **need** is for the*

*people I care about to receive the support they need to improve the quality of their lives. **What I want right now** is for him to tell me one of the four pieces of information about himself, his feelings.*

He responds, "Well, I'm just coming home in four months. I don't care what they say."

*He still hasn't told me anything about his **feelings** so I try a different route to the same goal. I guess his feelings.*

I ask, "Do you feel scared about being asked to stay longer than four months?"

"Yes," he says.

*In order to understand his fear the checklist suggests that I need to learn which of his **needs** is at stake,*

I ask, "What is it about staying longer than four months that disturbs you?"

"It's just too long," he says.

Open-ended questions often don't generate much information, so I take a different approach and try to guess what his relevant needs are.

I propose, "Does the idea of staying four months feel uncomfortable because you imagine that you will feel lonely being gone from home that long?"

He relaxes a bit and I see what looks like concern in his eyes. In a quieter voice he says, "Yes, I'll miss my family and friends, and it will be summer and I'll miss the beach."

It seems that his needs for companionship and to be in surroundings that he enjoys are the needs generating his fear, but I want to confirm that and let him know that I understand.

I ask, "When you think about four months do you worry that by then your needs for family, friends and fun surroundings will be so strong that you have trouble imagining how you will bare it?"

"Yes," he says softly. "I worry about that a lot."

Then I search for the fourth piece of information, is there anything he wants from me now?

I query, "Is there anything that you imagine I could do or say now that would help you feel better about this?"

"No," he says. "It's just something that I really worry about. I've never been gone from home that long."

At this point we have completed one cycle of communication. Each of us has been able to learn the four facts about the other as they are, at this moment, related to this issue. I could go on to offer him more empathy for his fear, or see if we can come up with some things that might help him with his fear, or see if he is willing to hear the dreams for wonderful personal growth and maturing that I am imagining he could realize by staying with the rehabilitation program. The important fact—the door to further communication is open.

☐

More Complex
Uses

Most of the time, I use the concepts and tools of Nonviolent Communication like a pilot's checklist. They help me maintain my focus on heart related issues—like people's well-being and how to improve it—rather than on analytical issues such as right, wrong or who's to blame. They help me remember the important points and critical tasks that tend to inspire compassion, connection and generosity in my relationships.

That is, Nonviolent Communication not only helps me resolve troubled communications, it also helps me avoid creating them in the first place. The following example demonstrates this.

When the Stakes or Pain Are High

When I know that I or the person I'm speaking with hurts intensely, or that our current needs are very compelling, I try to keep both what I think privately and say publicly in close alignment with the process' guidelines. I use both the checklist of four facts and the three recommendations like a pilot's checklist to help me create a climate where compassion and generosity might flourish.

A Family Example

The following is an imaginary conversation between a mother and her college age daughter. It shows how the mother might use Nonviolent Communication to help a compassionate connection while discussing an emotionally charged subject:

> Carol, who now lives across the country, announces, "Mom, it really upsets me that you want to get rid of our dog."
>
> *The mother hears intense emotions in Carol's voice and knows this dog is dear to her, so Mom*

decides to use the tools of Nonviolent Communication to help. She knows that she needs to get them both talking about how they are feeling in relation to this topic and what they need. Mom decides to use the checklist as a guide. She believes that she knows Carol's triggering event, so she identifies it as a way to confirm it, and then immediately focuses on learning the second piece of information, what Carol is feeling.

Mom asks, "Does hearing that I want to give Sparky to another family leave you feeling sad?"

"No, Mom, I'm really mad," Carol corrects.

Now that she knows Carol's emotion, anger, Mom begins to search for the needs Carol has which are creating that feeling.

Mom asks, "Are you angry because you care very much about Sparky and you want him to be well cared for by others, but you worry that he won't be?"

*Here, the mother has done something very special in the way she has expressed herself. Notice that as she searches for why Carol is angry **she keeps the focus on Carol** and on what Carol may be needing, but fearing she can't have.*

Mom doesn't speak as though anything she did or is planning to do created her daughter's emotions. Mom's actions may have served as a trigger, but Carol's emotions arose because Carol has needs (which will be clarified in a moment) that are related to what the mother is considering doing.

"No Mom," Carol says. "I am mad because he is part of our family and I don't want you to throw him out."

Mom replies, "Oh, so are you angry because you cherish Sparky and you want him to remain a cherished member of the family?"

*Mom is trying to refine her understanding of the specific needs **Carol has** that are producing Carol's emotions.*

Carol affirms Mom's guess. "Yeah, Mom, Sparky is a special family member just as much as we kids. You just don't give away family members."

Wanting to be sure that she understands Carol correctly, Mom tries a summary..

"You'd like Sparky to be given the same love and loyalty as the human family members and to remain a member of the family for as long as he lives?"

"Yes, that's right."

Having finally clarified Carol's most important need, Mom begins to share her feelings and needs.

"I appreciate your dream for Sparky to be given the same commitment as the human family members. At this time he and I live alone and I find myself feeling frustrated because I would like the freedom to come and go as I need and not worry about whether Sparky is safe, fed, comfortable, getting into trouble or whatever. For me, he is like a little child that can't grow up and with you children grown and gone I'd like to be free of all the parenting-like responsibilities that come along with caring for a dog. I am thinking it would be best for me if he could live with someone else."

*Having shared her feelings and their related needs, the second and third pieces of information, Mom moves on to the fourth —requesting what she wants from Carol right now, **in specific and doable terms**.*

"Do my feelings and needs make sense to you?"

"Yes, I understand. I really wish he could come and live with me. It's such a bummer that I live in a dorm."

Mom decides to offer some empathy.

"It sounds like you wish there were an easy, comfortable answer and feel sad that there isn't."

Carol responds, "Yah, real sad."

Mom empathizes again, "Sparky means a lot to you."

"Yah, he does."

Mom decides to try focusing on a part of Carol's needs that they might be able to satisfy.

"Well, if we can't fulfill the part of your desire to have Sparky live with us for the rest of his life, maybe we can fulfill the part where you want him to feel loved and cared for. Could you tell me if there is a way we can go about looking for a loving home for Sparky that would meet your need to believe he is loved and wanted?"

Carol answers, "Well, I just don't like the idea, but I see what you are needing and I don't see another way. I wish I did, but I don't. I guess that what I want is for you to do a really good job checking out whomever he might live with

64

and make sure that it is OK for me to visit when I'm home."

*Mom knows that Nonviolent Communication suggests that she get Carol to clarify, **in specific and doable terms**, what doing a "really good job" would mean to her. So Mom makes a guess.*

"Do you want me to see their house and yard, meet their kids, ask them why they want a dog, let Sparky meet them, see how he likes them and they him, etc.?"

"That's exactly what I want, Mom. And I want you to tell me about them and what you learned before you make a decision, and I want you to ask them if I can visit whenever I want."

At that point, Mom would probably say, "OK, I'll be glad to."

In this example, the mother helps guide the conversation in a constructive, compassionate and connection building direction by focusing on learning about Carol's feelings, what needs Carol has which are producing those feelings, and giving Carol the same information about herself.

This is a basic pattern in Nonviolent Communication. Carol is feeling angry, but beneath that she is afraid and perhaps sad. She cares for her dog very much and wants him to live with a family member for the rest of his life. Rather than commenting on whether Carol is good or bad for feeling as she does, and wanting what she wants, Mom works on clarifying her understanding of Carol's feelings and needs, and on giving Carol genuine empathy for them.

The resulting dialog helps both of them identify the most important needs they each have, and once those are clearly stated, together they begin to look for specific ways to proceed that would satisfy their needs. In this way, this example demonstrates the important phenomenon I spoke of earlier: if two people are willing to spend enough time clarifying their needs, don't confuse their needs with their requests, and don't prematurely move on to making their requests, then a mutually acceptable solution often takes shape naturally. I find this one of the most valuable concepts to remember.

When the Way I Speak
Disrupts the Communication

Sometimes the way I speak helps make the conversation spin rapidly downward and I feel bewildered and afraid. In these moments, if I can muster enough emotional detachment and objectivity, I use the checklist's four facts and the three recommendations to help me figure out why things are going poorly. These tools encourage me to check to see if the four pieces of information are the focus of our conversation and if we are speaking about them in the three suggested ways.

Using the checklist

I begin my problem solving by going through the checklist and asking myself:

① Do I know what **event** served as a trigger for the party I am speaking with, or, if I initiated the conversation, have I clearly identified my triggering event?

② Do I know what **emotions** others are feeling about this event and have I told them what mine are?

③ Have we both clearly identified which **personal needs** of ours are producing our feelings and are we adequately differentiating between our needs and requests?

④ Do we know **what each of us wants** to do, or have another do, **right now**, which might help us feel immediately more comfortable or content?

Expressed differently, what I'm interested in is the following:

○ Do I know where this conversation started?

○ Are we talking about our feelings and needs?

○ Are we confusing our requests with our needs?

○ And, do we each know what the other specifically wants to do, or have another do, *at this moment?*

Answering these questions helps me decide if our struggles are due to a missing or confused piece of information.

Using the three recommendations

If the four pieces of information are present and clear, then the process tells me to look next at how we are speaking about them. Are we following the three recommendations? We may be speaking in one or more of these disruptive ways;

1. **Name-calling and criticizing**: In some way telling each other what we think is right or wrong with the other or their behavior.

2. **Blaming**: Speaking as though someone other than ourselves has made us think, feel or act as we did or do.

3. **Bossing or Threatening**: In some way telling the other what he or she must, should, ought to, is supposed to, or had better do or not do.

These three ways of speaking almost always send my conversations into downward spirals. One way out is for me to bring my ways of speaking in line with the three recommendations as follows:

(1) **Describe** events, feelings and needs rather than express my moralistic opinions about them.

(2) **Illuminate** how **my needs** are producing my feelings and acknowledge that I have freely chosen to do what I'm doing.

(3) **Describe what I want next**, or clarify my understanding of what they want next, **in specific, doable terms**.

□

A Lover Example

The following is a conversation where a lover's way of talking disrupts the communication and shows how he can use the tools of the process to sort it out.

Tom starts a conversation with his girlfriend by saying, "I'm tired of being judged by you."

Confused and taken aback, Gail asks, "What do you mean ?

"I mean lately you've been criticizing me a lot."

In a weary voice Gail replies, "Tom, I'm worn out. Give me a break. I can't be perfect all the time."

Tom can feel their conversation beginning a sickening, familiar plummet, so he stops. He thinks about the Nonviolent Communication process and reviews what he's said, how he's said it, and what may be missing. Tom immediately sees that the pieces of information that the checklist suggests he talk about are missing. He hasn't told her what particular events he is responding to, what his emotions are, what unmet needs of his are generating those feelings, or what he'd like her to do right after he stops talking. He has omitted all four pieces of the

checklist's information. Amazing! He also sees
that he is speaking about his distress by telling
Gail what he thinks is wrong with her. This is
a fairly reliable way to start a pain-filled,
unproductive debate. So, he tries again.

"I'm sorry," Tom says, "I'm not doing this in a way that feels good. Let me start over. Last night, when I said I'd spent two and a half hours in the bookstore and found nothing I wanted, you responded with, 'Oh, if you go to that local bookstore, you'll never find anything there.' I had a hard time not hearing your statement as a criticism implying that I was a fool for going there, and that everyone else in our community knows better. In the last couple of days, we've had two or three similar exchanges. Being able to talk about my struggles and be heard with compassion and understanding is important to me. I'm starting to feel hesitant to tell you what I've done for fear that my worth is going to be measured and I'll be found wanting."

He has now shared his triggering events with her,
the feelings that were spawned, and which of
his needs and beliefs produced his emotions.

Gail replies quickly, "Well I didn't mean to put you down."

"Wait," Tom protests. "I don't want you to apologize."

He realizes that he did not tell her what he **would like** *from her right now, so he proceeds to do so.*

"My first desire is to know if you can recall that conversation last night."

"Yes," Gail replies.

"OK, great," he says. "It's just an example and I don't really need to focus on it. I only bring it up so you can know that in the last few days I've been feeling insecure, self-doubting and scared so that when I believe somebody's criticizing me it hits me hard. Right now, I want to share with you what's been going on in me that leads me to feel unsure of myself. I need more to talk about the pain of that insecurity, and receive empathy for it, than to discuss your actions."

And then he ends by making a specific request for what he'd like next.

"I'd like to know what you are feeling as you hear me say this."

Gail responds, "Relieved. Relieved and concerned. I didn't know you were in special pain lately."

At this point, they might move into a fruitful and relief producing exploration of his distress, possibly followed by an exploration of her stress and fatigue.

Using the tools of Nonviolent Communication Tom figures out what he is doing that contributes to this conversation going awry and how to change it. By foregoing blaming and accusation, and instead concentrating on describing his feelings and needs, the conversation not only goes in a new direction, but shifts tone entirely. It goes from being characterized by fear, anger and shame, to being characterized by concern, compassion and a willingness to help.

For me, using the tools of Nonviolent Communication to help make such a transformation takes determination, energy and a sufficient amount of awareness and objectivity about my emotions. I continue to work at it because I find it immensely helpful.

When I Am Disturbed
by the Way They Speak

When people try to tell me that they are in pain
by telling me what they think is wrong with me,
or try to explain why they are feeling bad by
pointing to something I've done, or try to ask
for what they want by telling me what I ought
or must do, I often become incensed. I don't
like thinking I'm being criticized, blamed or
bossed. I quickly feel a mixture of anger, fear
and embarrassment, and then the desire to
defend, attack, bolt or revolt.

   When I start feeling these ways I rapidly lose
my ability to continue hearing the other's feelings and needs, and I begin dreaming of doing
things to them which will probably make the
conversation more miserable. In fact, if I don't
catch myself quickly, I can begin treating them
in exactly the same pain producing ways they
are treating me.

   In these situations I know from experience to
use the tools of Nonviolent Communication to
help me figure out what I'm needing that I'm
not getting and how to ask for it.

I usually wish that they would express themselves in ways that are more compassionate, i.e. in line with the three recommendations, and I want them to tell me about their triggering events, their feelings, needs and requests. Let's look at an example where one person's way of speaking sets another off and what the distressed person does internally and externally to cope with and redirect the conversation. (This example appears longer than the others because I want to give you a lot of information about what goes on in the heart and mind of the person trying to use the tools of Nonviolent Communication to deal with a conversation that strongly disturbs him or her.)

A Business Example

Phil and Ted are business partners. Along with others, they own various pieces of investment real estate.

Ted starts the conversation by saying to Phil, "When we put our office building on the market you had a fiduciary responsibility to negotiate the lowest possible sales commission for the partnership. By making a deal whereby we had to pay a six percent commission, rather than the customary five, you utterly failed to perform your fiduciary duty. If you had to give up your one percent commission share in order to get us five percent, you should have. The commission you received should be refunded to the partnership and you should trust us to pay you what is fair for the work you did on our behalf."

Phil becomes quite disturbed. He has a hard time not believing that he's being told that he is incompetent, lacks sufficient integrity and that a lot of hard work may go without reward. Thinking these things, Phil produces anger within himself, fury as a matter of fact, and he wants revenge. He immediately loses any interest in being concerned about what Ted is feeling, needing or wanting. All he wants is to attack and hurl something at Ted like, "Up yours, you arrogant jerk. How dare you! You have no idea what you're talking about. You have no idea how much work was involved and how much money I was able to save and earn for the partners. Forget it."

In the past, Phil has acted on impulses like this and he remembers what usually happens—both people escalate their accusations, invectives and name-calling and only end up feeling more miserable and much farther from resolution. So Phil pauses a moment and assesses what's been happening.

The first thing he notices is that each of them is now very upset. From experience he knows that when each side has strong feelings then he needs to make a choice about whose feelings and needs get focused on first. He usually tries to guess who has either the greatest pain, or the lowest capacity to tolerate their pain, and see if he can get them to speak first. Phil knows that his anger is mostly triggered by the words Ted is using and that Ted is very upset by the issues. Phil decides to focus more on Ted's feelings, but only after he uses Nonviolent Communication's checklist and recommendations to let Ted know how his choice of words is affecting him.

Phil says, "Ted, when I hear phrases like 'failed responsibility' and 'you should,' all I want to do is fight because my integrity and freedom are important to me and I believe they are both being challenged. But, I don't think fighting will get us where we'd like to go. Would you be willing to tell me how you wanted the commission to be handled?"

> *Here Phil is doing two things. First, he is using Nonviolent Communication to tell Ted what Ted is specifically doing that Phil's reacting to, how he is reacting emotionally and why, and what he would like from Ted instead. And second, by asking Ted how he wanted the commission handled, Phil is using the first recommendation by trying to get Ted to talk about activities people could perform, rather than Ted's opinions of Phil's character.*

Ted responds, "I wanted you to act with more fiduciary integrity."

> *"Fiduciary integrity" is a moralistic concept that can trigger defensiveness and debate, rather than an activity someone can perform. Therefore, Phil responds, :*

"OK, but can you tell me precisely how I needed to act in order to demonstrate more 'fiduciary integrity' to you?"

"Yes," Ted says. "I wanted you to bargain harder to get your share out of a five percent total commission and if the realtor you thought was the best sales agent for the partnership wasn't willing to share one percent of his five percent with you then you should have worked for whatever you could get. There was very little work for you to do anyway. I know because I've represented the partnership during previous property sales."

With the exception of his last sentence, Ted is now mostly speaking in terms of behaviors he wanted, instead of evaluations he's making, so they are progressing. Phil imagines that if he responds to Ted's last sentence, then they will launch off into a new debate and since he wants to stay with his original question, Phil ignores the last sentence and tries to confirm what he thought he heard.

"Did you want the sale's commission paid by the partnership to be set as low as possible first and for my compensation to be negotiated second?"

"Yes," Ted responds, "that's exactly what I wanted. That would have been fairest for the partnership."

Ted's use of the word "fairest" is another invitation to debate, but since this isn't an issue Phil

wants to debate, Phil lets it pass like a speeding car .

Phil knows from experience that the first thing that hurt or frightened people usually want is to hear that someone understands their pain or fear.

So he says, "I know that you wanted the total amount of the sales commission negotiated to its lowest point first and for me to see if I could negotiate anything for myself after that, but I have two problems with that method. Would you be willing to hear what they are?"

"Yes," Ted says.

Phil goes on, "It violates my sense of integrity to sit with a realtor and try to negotiate their sales commission down to the lowest point he or she is willing to accept without letting that person know that I am going to expect them to share some of their commission with me. It appears to me like I am trying to trick them and that doesn't feel good."

Ted rejoins, "I don't care whether it feels good. It's the way business is done."

Phil replies, "I agree that some people are comfortable doing business that way, but I am not. My way of thinking is that the services needed to sell this property include not only the realtor's, but my services as the partnership's representative. It is customary for the selling party to pay for the services needed to sell a property and I feel better being open about the need for me to be compensated and negotiating their commission and my share at the same time. If I did it the way I understand you wanted it done, at one moment I would be telling the realtor that they must settle for a certain amount in order to get the contract, and then after they've committed, I would proceed to tell them, 'No, you must give up more if you want the contract.' I find that very uncomfortable because it violates my sense of fairness."

Phil wants to be sure he is understood in the way he desires so he ends by making a request.

"In your own words, can you tell me what problem you hear I'm struggling with?"

At this point, using the tools of Nonviolent Communication, Phil has shifted their conversation away from being a debate over each other's opinions or evaluations and into being a discussion of the pros and cons of different ways of handling this negotiation. If this conversation were to proceed, he would probably keep encouraging them to discuss *how they wanted things to be done* rather than *their opinions* of each other's behavior or values. Debating opinions and values can be done endlessly, whereas by discussing different *ways to act*, they might develop a mutually acceptable method they could use in the future.

□

A Long-term Benefit of Practicing Nonviolent Communication

I hope these examples, and the book as a whole, have conveyed some of why I value Nonviolent Communication so highly. And, there is one more benefit I want to describe.

I have found that as people use the tools and concepts regularly a gradual transition often takes place: They begin to relate to themselves and others from a more compassionate awareness that is born out of their repeated discovery that in everything each of us does we are all motivated by the same deep need—the need to sustain or improve the quality or continuity of our lives.

In response to this recognition people often become less interested in categorizing themselves and others, that is, deciding *what* and *how* worthy people are, and more interested in speaking to and from the heart—learning *how* people are, what they need and how to provide it.

Over time, as a result of this gradual shift in attitude and behavior, people often begin to **learn how to live from, and inspire in others,**

a compassion infused state of heart, mind and action from which misunderstanding, alienation and violence occur less often. Perhaps this compassion infused state of heart and mind will be the subject for an intermediate primer.

☐

Conclusion

Marshall Rosenberg's Nonviolent Communication process provides me with a deeply compassionate perspective for relating to myself and
others and with the best communication tools
I've found. His insights and tools help me know
how to listen, think and speak in ways that not
only increase understanding and rapport, but
also enhance people's respect for each other's
differences and heighten their interest in working together to realize individual and communal
dreams.

Becoming proficient in the Nonviolent
Communication process has involved a lot of
trial, error and practice. I have found it difficult
to learn how to listen, think and speak in ways
so different from my culture's. I am grateful for
my perseverance, my willingness to risk embar-

rassment and just do the best I can and for the support I've received as more and more of my friends and colleagues have committed to learning these skills.

I hope that I have shared my understanding and use of Nonviolent Communication in ways that leave you feeling eager and sufficiently confident to begin using its principles in your lives. I am certain that if you will brave any awkwardness encountered, you will enjoy the same healing, heartwarming and community-building benefits I have. I wish you well.

□

My Favorite Tips

When someone has expressed some sort of pain and you are not sure what they want you to do, *don't* immediately problem solve. Instead, empathize. Imaginatively guess what they might be feeling and how it relates to what they need, then share your guesses with them. (Don't worry about guessing "wrong." The fact that you try at all is a gift in itself.) When their most important feelings and needs have been reflected back to them they will usually relax a bit. Empathize until you see that relaxation, then talk about solutions if you still need or want to.

Needs never refer to specific other people. Requests do. Be careful not to confuse your basic need, or another's basic need, with your requests for *when, where, how, how much and by whom* you each want your needs to be met.

When faced with anger, ask yourself, "What is this person needing or wanting that they haven't received or fear losing?" Share your guesses with them.

When your conversations start to become unmanageable, pause, break away for a moment, then use the checklist and three recommendations as assessment and solution guides to help you identify any changes in language or approach that might help. You can ask yourself, "Have I been talking about *my* behavior, *my* feelings and *my* needs, or have I been analyzing, blaming, categorizing or labeling the *other person's* behavior, feelings and needs?"

When in doubt, empathize. If another stops speaking and you don't know what they want from you, it is usually safe to just empathize — share with them your perceptions of what they are feeling and how it relates to what they are needing.

□

A Request

If in some special way you enjoy this book or wish it were different, I'd love to hear from you. If you respond, please be specific about what you like or wish was different.

Contact Information

Wayland Myers, Ph.D.
645 Cole Ranch Road
Encinitas, CA, USA, 92024

Telephone: 760-688-8201
Email: waylandpm@cox.net

The Center for Nonviolent Communication is an international non-profit 501(c)(3) organization founded by Marshall Rosenberg. It offers training in Nonviolent Communication.
For information about training and support materials please contact the Center at:

U.S. Orders: 800-255-7696
International Orders: 505-244-4041
Email: bookstore@cnvc.org
Internet: http://cnvc.org